FERDINAND "JELLY ROLL" MORTON

STOP AND GO

Jazz Orchestra

Edited by
JAMES DAPOGNY

B♭ Tenor Saxophone 1

Published by C.F. Peters on behalf of The Historic New Orleans Collection.

C.F. PETERS CORPORATION
A member of the EDITION PETERS GROUP
LEIPZIG · LONDON · NEW YORK

Tenor Sax. 1

STOP AND GO

Composed and arranged by
Ferdinand "Jelly Roll" Morton
Edited by James Dapogny

Edition Peters 68488a

FERDINAND "JELLY ROLL" MORTON

STOP AND GO

Jazz Orchestra

Edited by
JAMES DAPOGNY

B♭ Tenor Saxophone 2

Published by C.F. Peters on behalf of The Historic New Orleans Collection.

C.F. PETERS CORPORATION
A member of the EDITION PETERS GROUP
LEIPZIG · LONDON · NEW YORK

Tenor Sax. 2

STOP AND GO

Composed and arranged by
Ferdinand "Jelly Roll" Morton
Edited by James Dapogny

Edition Peters 68488a

FERDINAND "JELLY ROLL" MORTON

STOP AND GO

Jazz Orchestra

Edited by

JAMES DAPOGNY

B♭ Trumpet 1

Published by C.F. Peters on behalf of The Historic New Orleans Collection.

C.F. PETERS CORPORATION

A member of the EDITION PETERS GROUP

LEIPZIG · LONDON · NEW YORK

Trumpet in B♭ 1

Stop and Go

Composed and arranged by
Ferdinand "Jelly Roll" Morton
Edited by James Dapogny

FERDINAND "JELLY ROLL" MORTON

STOP AND GO

Jazz Orchestra

Edited by

JAMES DAPOGNY

Bb Trumpet 2

Published by C.F. Peters on behalf of The Historic New Orleans Collection.

EIGENTUM DES VERLEGERS · ALLE RECHTE VORBEHALTEN

ALL RIGHTS RESERVED

C.F. PETERS CORPORATION

A member of the EDITION PETERS GROUP

LEIPZIG · LONDON · NEW YORK

Trumpet in B♭ 2

Stop and Go

Composed and arranged by
Ferdinand "Jelly Roll" Morton
Edited by James Dapogny

4

Trumpet in B♭ 2

FERDINAND "JELLY ROLL" MORTON

STOP AND GO

Jazz Orchestra

Edited by
JAMES DAPOGNY

B♭ Trumpet 3

Published by C.F. Peters on behalf of The Historic New Orleans Collection.

C.F. PETERS CORPORATION
A member of the EDITION PETERS GROUP
LEIPZIG · LONDON · NEW YORK

Trumpet in B♭ 3

Stop and Go

Composed and arranged by
Ferdinand "Jelly Roll" Morton
Edited by James Dapogny

FERDINAND "JELLY ROLL" MORTON

STOP AND GO

Jazz Orchestra

Edited by
JAMES DAPOGNY

Trombone 1

Published by C.F. Peters on behalf of The Historic New Orleans Collection.

EIGENTUM DES VERLEGERS · ALLE RECHTE VORBEHALTEN

C.F. PETERS CORPORATION
A member of the EDITION PETERS GROUP

LEIPZIG · LONDON · NEW YORK

Trombone 1

Stop and Go

Composed and arranged by
Ferdinand "Jelly Roll" Morton
Edited by James Dapogny

Edition Peters 68488a

FERDINAND "JELLY ROLL" MORTON

STOP AND GO

Jazz Orchestra

Edited by
JAMES DAPOGNY

Trombone 2

Published by C.F. Peters on behalf of The Historic New Orleans Collection.

EIGENTUM DES VERLEGERS · ALLE RECHTE VORBEHALTEN

ALL RIGHTS RESERVED

C.F. PETERS CORPORATION

A member of the EDITION PETERS GROUP

LEIPZIG · LONDON · NEW YORK

Trombone 2

STOP AND GO

Composed and arranged by
Ferdinand "Jelly Roll" Morton
Edited by James Dapogny

Edition Peters 68488a

FERDINAND "JELLY ROLL" MORTON

STOP AND GO

Jazz Orchestra

Edited by
JAMES DAPOGNY

E♭ Alto Saxophone 1

Published by C.F. Peters on behalf of The Historic New Orleans Collection.

C.F. PETERS CORPORATION
A member of the EDITION PETERS GROUP
LEIPZIG · LONDON · NEW YORK

Alto Sax. 1

Stop and Go

Composed and arranged by
Ferdinand "Jelly Roll" Morton
Edited by James Dapogny

FERDINAND "JELLY ROLL" MORTON

STOP AND GO

Jazz Orchestra

Edited by
JAMES DAPOGNY

E♭ Alto Saxophone 2

Published by C.F. Peters on behalf of The Historic New Orleans Collection.

EIGENTUM DES VERLEGERS · ALLE RECHTE VORBEHALTEN

ALL RIGHTS RESERVED

C.F. PETERS CORPORATION

A member of the EDITION PETERS GROUP

LEIPZIG · LONDON · NEW YORK

Alto Sax. 2

STOP AND GO

Composed and arranged by
Ferdinand "Jelly Roll" Morton
Edited by James Dapogny

Edition Peters 68488a

FERDINAND "JELLY ROLL" MORTON

STOP AND GO

Jazz Orchestra

Edited by
JAMES DAPOGNY

Trombone 3

Published by C.F. Peters on behalf of The Historic New Orleans Collection.

EIGENTUM DES VERLEGERS · ALLE RECHTE VORBEHALTEN

ALL RIGHTS RESERVED

C.F. PETERS CORPORATION
A member of the EDITION PETERS GROUP
LEIPZIG · LONDON · NEW YORK

Trombone 3

STOP AND GO

Composed and arranged by
Ferdinand "Jelly Roll" Morton
Edited by James Dapogny

FERDINAND "JELLY ROLL" MORTON

STOP AND GO

Jazz Orchestra

Edited by
JAMES DAPOGNY

Piano

Published by C.F. Peters on behalf of The Historic New Orleans Collection.

C.F. PETERS CORPORATION

A member of the EDITION PETERS GROUP

LEIPZIG · LONDON · NEW YORK

Piano

STOP AND GO

Composed and arranged by
Ferdinand "Jelly Roll" Morton
Edited by James Dapogny

Edition Peters 68488a

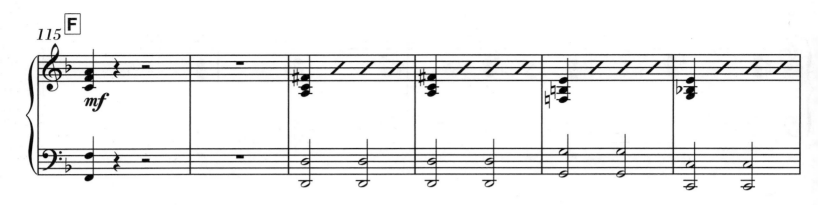

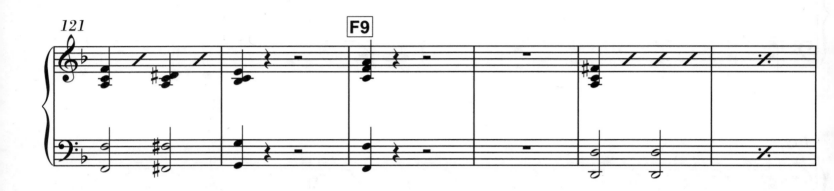

FERDINAND "JELLY ROLL" MORTON

STOP AND GO

Jazz Orchestra

Edited by
JAMES DAPOGNY

Guitar

Published by C.F. Peters on behalf of The Historic New Orleans Collection.

EIGENTUM DES VERLEGERS · ALLE RECHTE VORBEHALTEN

ALL RIGHTS RESERVED

C.F. PETERS CORPORATION

A member of the EDITION PETERS GROUP

LEIPZIG · LONDON · NEW YORK

Guitar

Stop and Go

Composed and arranged by
Ferdinand "Jelly Roll" Morton
Edited by James Dapogny

Edition Peters 68488a

* In Morton's part this is written as two quarter note strokes.
The editor believes that Morton would have had the guitarist play this as notated here.

FERDINAND "JELLY ROLL" MORTON

STOP AND GO

Jazz Orchestra

Edited by
JAMES DAPOGNY

Bass

Published by C.F. Peters on behalf of The Historic New Orleans Collection.

C.F. PETERS CORPORATION
A member of the EDITION PETERS GROUP
LEIPZIG · LONDON · NEW YORK

Bass

STOP AND GO

Composed and arranged by
Ferdinand "Jelly Roll" Morton
Edited by James Dapogny

FERDINAND "JELLY ROLL" MORTON

STOP AND GO

Jazz Orchestra

Edited by
JAMES DAPOGNY

Drum Set

Published by C.F. Peters on behalf of The Historic New Orleans Collection.

EIGENTUM DES VERLEGERS · ALLE RECHTE VORBEHALTEN

ALL RIGHTS RESERVED

C.F. PETERS CORPORATION

A member of the EDITION PETERS GROUP

LEIPZIG · LONDON · NEW YORK

Drum Set

STOP AND GO

Composed and arranged by
Ferdinand "Jelly Roll" Morton
Edited by James Dapogny

Edition Peters 68488a